ILLINOIS
Responsible Vendor Training Guide

A Comprehensive Guide for Cannabis Dispensary Compliance and Safety

ACC OF ILLINOIS
APPROVED BY THE ILLINOIS DEPARTMENT OF
FINANCIAL AND PROFESSIONAL REGULATION TO PROVIDE

This 2024 Illinois Responsible Vendor Training Guide is your comprehensive resource for mastering cannabis dispensary compliance. Covering everything from health and safety standards to detailed Illinois state laws, this guide equips dispensary staff, managers, and agents-in-charge with the essential knowledge for safe, legal, and effective cannabis operations.

Topics Included:

- Inventory tracking and compliance -

- ID verification and minor sale prohibitions -

- Packaging, labeling, and security standards -

- Waste disposal and public safety measures -

Follow ACC on Instagram @ACCOFILLINOIS

ACC Of Illinois Responsible Vendor Training Program

APPROVED BY:
The Illinois Department of Financial and Professional Regulations.

@ ACCOFILLINOIS
Approved by IDFPR & IL Dept of Agr

What topics must be covered in my training module?

Training modules must include training on:

- Health and safety concerns of cannabis use, including the responsible use of cannabis, its Physical effects, onset of physiological effects, recognizing signs of impairment, and appropriate responses in the event of overconsumption;
- Laws and regulations on driving while under the influence;
- Sales to minor prohibitions;
- All relevant Illinois laws and rules:
- Acceptable forms of identification, including how to check identification and common mistakes made in verification;
- Safe storage of cannabis;
- Compliance with all inventory tracking regulations;
- Waste handline, management, and disposal;
- Health and safety standards at the dispensary;
- Maintenance of records;
- Security and surveillance requirements;
- Permitting inspections by State and local licensing and enforcement authorities;
- Privacy issues; and
- Packaging and labeling requirements

What topics must be covered in my training module?

Who needs to receive training from a Responsible Vendor?

All owners, managers, employees, and agents involved in the handling or sale of cannabis or cannabis-infused products employed by an adult use dispensing organization or medical cannabis dispensing organization as defined in Section 10 of the Compassionate Use of Medical Cannabis Program Act.

Are all Principal Officers required to receive training from a Responsible Vendor?

The only agents that are required to receive the Responsible Vendor Training are those involved in the handling or sale of cannabis or cannabis-infused products. However, all agents, including all Principal Officers, must meet the 8-hour training requirement found in Section 15-65(a)(5) of the Cannabis Regulation and Tax Act.

Can a Responsible Vendor provide all 8 hours of the training required by Section 15-65(a)(5)?

Yes, provided the training meets all the requirements of Section 15-406)(3) and 15-65(a)(5) of the Cannabis Regulation and Tax Act.

What topics must be covered in my training module?

Does the training provided by the Responsible Vendor count toward the 8-hour training required by Section 15-65(a)(5)?

Yes. For example, if the Responsible Vendor training is for 3 hours. A dispensing organization would still be required to provide 5 hours of 3 additional training per year. In any case, a dispensary agent, agent-in-charge, and principal officer must receive training on the following topics as prescribed by Section 15-65(a)(5) of the Cannabis Regulation and Tax Act: (i) how to effectively operate the point-of-sale system and the State's verification system, (i) proper inventory handling and tracking, (iii) specific uses of cannabis or cannabis-infused products, (iv) instruction regarding regulatory inspection preparedness and law enforcement interaction, and (v) awareness of the legal requirements for maintaining status as an agent.

When must individuals receive the training from a Responsible Vendor?

The training must be received within 90 days of September 1, 2019 or within 90 days before or after the first day of employment at a dispensary, whichever is later. Training received outside of the 90-day window will not meet the training requirement imposed by Section 15-40(i) of the Cannabis Regulation and Tax Act.

How often must individuals receive training from a Responsible Vendor?

Training must be received annually.

ACC Of Illinois Responsible Vendors Training Program

- Public Safety
- Legalities
- Dispensary Operation
- Cannabis Usage Basics
- Handling Cannabis

Table of Contents

Laws & Rules For Adult Dispensary Agents............................10
Laws And Rules For Dispensing Cannabis............................11
Verification Process..12
Quantity Limitations..13
ID Basics 14
Consumer Safety 15
Minor Sale Prohibition, Rules & Laws 16
Possession Of Adult Use Cannabis In A Motor Vehicle. 17
Public Safety 19
Health & Safety Standards At Dispensary 20
Security, Storage, Inventory, And Distribution Of Cannabis. 22
Dispensary Operations 24
Inventory Tracking System Regulations 25
Security And Surveillance Requirements 26
Privacy Issues 27
Handling the Cannabis 29
Packaging & Labeling Requirements 30
Safe Storage Of Cannabis 31
Waste Handling, Management & Disposal 32
Cannabis Usage 33
Health & Safety Concerns Of Cannabis Use 34
Keep Children Safe 35
Physical And Psychological Effects 36
Test Your Skills 37
Multiple-Choice Questions 38
Answer Sheet 39
In The Event of Emergency..40

Laws & Rules For Adult Dispensary Agents
Laws & Rules For Dispensing Cannabis
Quantity Limitations
Acceptable Forms Of Identification (Id)

- Overview

- The objective is for students to be able to understand and explain all laws and rules for dispensary agents to know and perform daily functions. Walk through all forms of acceptable id, including how to check identification and common mistakes made in verification.

Laws & Rules For Adult Dispensary Agents

A. Every dispensing organization shall designate, at a minimum, one agent-in-charge for each licensed dispensary. The designated agent-in-charge must hold a dispensing organization agent identification card.

B. The agent-in-charge shall be a principal officer or a full-time agent of the dispensing organization and shall manage the dispensary. Managing the dispensary includes, but is not limited to, responsibility for opening and closing the dispensary, delivery acceptance, oversight of sales and dispensing organization agents, recordkeeping, inventory, dispensing organization agent training, and compliance with this Act and rules. Participation in affairs also includes the responsibility for maintaining all files subject to audit or inspection by the Department at the dispensary.

The agent-in-charge is responsible for notifying the Department of a change in the employment status of all dispensing organization agents within 5 business days after the change, including notice to the Department if the termination of an agent was for diversion of product or theft of currency.

C. The dispensing organization agent-in-charge registration shall expire one year from the date it is issued

D. Upon termination of an agent-in-charge's employment, the dispensing organization shall immediately reclaim the dispensing agent identification card. The dispensing organization shall promptly return the identification card to the Department.

Laws & Rules For Dispensing Cannabis

- Quantity Limitations
- Acceptable Forms Of ID
- Verification Process

Verification Process

Before a dispensing organization agent dispenses cannabis to a purchaser, the agent shall:

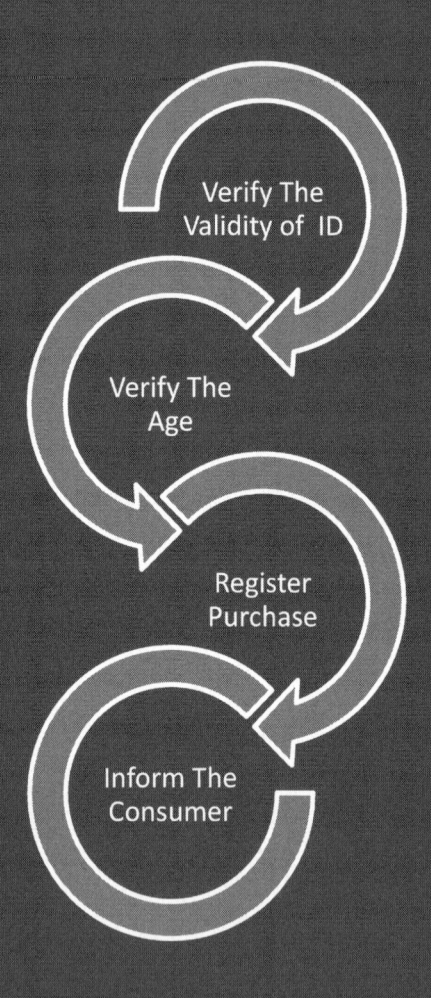

- Verify The Validity of ID
- Verify The Age
- Register Purchase
- Inform The Consumer

Quantity Limitations

Illinois Residents

- ✓ **30** grams of cannabis flower
- ✓ No more than **500** milligrams of THC contained in cannabis-infused product
- ✓ **5** grams of cannabis concentrate

Non-Illinois Residents

- ✓ **15** grams of cannabis flower
- ✓ No more than **250** milligrams of THC contained in cannabis-infused product
- ✓ **2.5** grams of cannabis concentrate

ID Basics

Acceptable forms of ID include the following:

- ✓ A valid current driver's license or photo ID card issued by the Illinois Secretary of State's office or any other state.
- ✓ A valid Armed Forces ID
- ✓ A valid U.S. passport or foreign passport (with U.S. travel visa)
- ✓ Foid cards

A valid ID must include:

- ✓ Individuals Full Name
- ✓ Photograph and Date of Birth of Person
- ✓ Be valid and unexpired
- ✓ Current Address
- ✓ Date of Birth that indicates age of 21 or older in good condition (no cracks, chips, damage or inability to read essential information)
- ✓ Security formatting associated with that particular form of ID (seal, watermark, logo, paper type)

Consumer Safety

The objective is for students to be able to understand and explain laws and regulations associated with driving while under the influence of cannabis. Review laws and regulations associated with driving while under the influence of cannabis.

Minor Sale Prohibition, Rules & Laws

According to the Illinois House Bill 1438 In the interest of the health and public safety of the residents of Illinois, the General Assembly further finds and declares that cannabis should be regulated in a manner similar to alcohol so that:

- ✓ Persons will have to show proof of age
- ✓ Unless authorized by the Compassionate Use of Medical Cannabis Pilot Program Act or by the Community College Cannabis Vocational Pilot Program, no one under 21 can possess, purchase, or consume cannabis it is illegal
- ✓ No minors permitted on dispensing premises unless the minor is a minor qualifying patient under the Compassionate Use of Medical Cannabis Pilot Program Act
- ✓ Packaging and advertising must not contain information that depicts a person under 21 years of age

Possession of Adult Use Cannabis In A Motor Vehicle

- Driving under the influence of cannabis shall remain illegal
- It's illegal to operate a motor vehicle while under the influence of cannabis
- Any person who knowingly violates the laws above, in this section commits a Class A misdemeanor.
- Operating, navigating, or being in actual physical control of any motor vehicle, aircraft, or motorboat while using or under the influence of cannabis in violation of Section 11-501 or 11-502.1 of the Illinois Vehicle Code
- **"If the person under the age of 21 was in a motor vehicle at the time of the offense, the Secretary of State may suspend or revoke the driving privileges of any person for a violation of this Section under Section 6-206 of the Illinois Vehicle Code and the rules adopted under it."**

Possession of Adult Use Cannabis In A Motor Vehicle

- No driver, who is a medical cannabis cardholder, may use medical cannabis within the passenger area of any motor vehicle upon a highway in this state.
- No driver, who is a medical cannabis cardholder, a medical cannabis designated caregiver, medical cannabis cultivation center agent, or dispensing organization agent may possess medical cannabis within any area of any motor vehicle upon a highway in this state except in a sealed, odor-proof, and child resistant tamper-evident medical cannabis container
- No passenger, who is a medical cannabis card holder, a medical cannabis designated caregiver, or medical cannabis dispensing organization agent may possess medical cannabis within any passenger area of any motor vehicle upon a highway in this state except in a sealed, odor-proof, and child resistant tamper-evident medical cannabis container.

Public Safety

The objective is for students to be able to discuss health and safety standards, waste handling, management and disposal, including specifying that destruction shall always be done in the clear view of a camera.

Health & Safety Standards At Dispensary

No cannabis business establishment nor any other person or entity shall engage in advertising that contains any statement or illustration that are of the following:

- False or misleading
- Promotes over consumption of cannabis or cannabis products
- Depicts the actual consumption of cannabis or cannabis products
- Depicts a person under 21 years of age consuming cannabis
- Includes the image of a cannabis leaf or bud
- Makes any health, medicinal, or therapeutic claims about cannabis or cannabis-infused products
- Includes any image designed or likely to appeal to minors, including cartoons, toys, animals, or children, or any other likeness to images, characters, or phrases that is designed in any manner to be appealing to or encourage consumption of persons under 21 years of age.

Health & Safety Standards At Dispensary

No cannabis business establishment nor any other person or entity shall place or maintain, or cause to be placed or maintained, an advertisement of cannabis or a cannabis-infused product in any form or through any medium:

- Within 1,000 feet of the perimeter of school grounds, a playground, a recreation center or facility, a child care center, a public park or public library, or a game arcade to which admission is not restricted to persons 21 years of age or older
- On or in a public transit vehicle or public transit shelter
- On or in publicly owned or publicly operated property
- Contains information that is false or misleading
- Promotes excessive consumption
- Depicts a person under 21 years of age consuming cannabis
- Includes the image of a cannabis leaf

Security, Storage, Inventory, And Distribution of Cannabis

- A dispensing organization shall establish, maintain, and comply with written policies and procedures as submitted in the business, financial and operating plan as required. These policies and procedures shall include methods for identifying, recording, and reporting diversion, theft, or loss, and for correcting errors and inaccuracies in inventories.

- Mandatory and voluntary recalls of cannabis products. The policies shall be adequate to deal with recalls due to any action initiated at the request of the department and any voluntary action by the dispensing organization to remove defective or potentially defective cannabis from the market or any action undertaken to promote public health and safety

Security, Storage, Inventory, And Distribution of Cannabis

A. A mechanism reasonably calculated to contact purchasers who have, or likely have, obtained the product from the dispensary, including information on the policy for return of the recalled product;

B. A mechanism to identify and contact the adult use cultivation center, craft grower, or infuser that manufactured the cannabis;

C. Policies for communicating with the department, the department of agriculture, and the department of public health within 24 hours of discovering defective or potentially defective cannabis;

D. Policies for destruction of any recalled cannabis product;

Dispensary Operations

The objective is for students to be able to discuss and review how to properly maintain records required by the division and explain surveillance requirements, including notifying trainees that the division and Illinois state police have 24-hour access to cameras in the dispensary. Explain and review privacy issues related to all purchasers including purchasers who may be discussing medical issues.

Inventory Tracking System Regulations

- ❖ A dispensing organization agent-in-charge shall have primary oversight of the dispensing organization's cannabis inventory verification system, and its point-of-sale system. The inventory point-of-sale system shall be real-time, web-based, and accessible by the Department at any time. The point-of-sale system shall track, at a minimum the date of sale, amount, price, and currency.
- ❖ A dispensing organization shall establish an account with the State's verification system that documents
- ❖ Upon cannabis delivery, a dispensing organization shall confirm the product's name, strain name, weight, and identification number on the manifest matches the information on the cannabis product label and package. The product name listed and the weight listed in the State's verification system shall match the product packaging.
- ❖ The agent-in-charge shall conduct daily inventory reconciliation documenting and balancing cannabis inventory by confirming the State's verification system matches the dispensing organization's point-of-sale system and the amount of physical product at the dispensary

Security And Surveillance Requirements

The dispensing organization shall implement security measures to protect the premises, purchasers, and dispensing organization agents including, but not limited to the following:

- Establish a locked door or barrier between the facility's entrance and the limited access area
- Prevent individuals from remaining on the premises if they are not engaging in activity permitted by this Act or rules
- Develop a policy that addresses the maximum capacity and purchaser flow in the waiting rooms and limited access areas
- Dispose of cannabis in accordance with this Act and rules
- A dispensing organization shall implement security measures to deter and prevent entry into and theft of cannabis or currency
- A dispensing organization shall submit any changes to the floor plan or security plan to the Department for pre-approval. All cannabis shall be maintained and stored in a restricted access area during construction.

Privacy Issues

Information provided by the cannabis business establishment licensees or applicants to the department of agriculture, the department of public health, the department of financial and professional regulation, the department of commerce and economic opportunity, or other agency shall be limited to information necessary for the purposes of administering this act.

Privacy Issues

The following information received and records kept by the department of agriculture, the department of public health, the department of state police, and the department of financial and professional regulation for purposes of administering this article are subject to all applicable federal privacy laws, are confidential and exempt from disclosure under the freedom of information act, except as provided in this act, and not subject to disclosure to any individual or public or private entity, except to the department of financial and professional regulation, the department of agriculture, the department of public health, and the department of state police as necessary to perform official duties under this article. The following information received and kept by the department of financial and professional regulation or the department of agriculture, excluding any existing or non-existing Illinois or national criminal history record information, may be disclosed to the department of public health, the department of agriculture, the department of revenue, or the department of state police upon request:

Handling the Cannabis

The objective is for students to be able to discuss, review, and walk through packaging and labeling requirements for sales to purchasers. Review storage requirements and discuss the state's inventory system and inventory tracking process.

Packaging & Labeling Requirements

Packaging must not contain information that:

Is false or misleading

Promotes excessive consumption

Depicts a person under 21 years of age consuming cannabis

Packaging must have a use-by date and the weight of the contents

Safe Storage Of Cannabis

- Authorized on-premises storage. A dispensing organization must store inventory on its premises. All inventory stored on the premises must be secured in a restricted access area and tracked consistently with the inventory tracking rules.
- A dispensary shall be of suitable size and construction to facilitate cleaning, maintenance, and proper operations.
- A dispensary shall maintain adequate lighting., ventilation, temperature, humidity control, and equipment.
- Containers storing cannabis that have been tampered with, damaged, or opened shall be labelled with the date opened and quarantined from other cannabis products in the vault until they are disposed.

Waste Handling, Management & Disposal

- Cannabis and cannabis-infused products must be destroyed by rendering them unusable using methods approved by the Department that comply with this Act and rules.
- Cannabis waste rendered unusable must be promptly disposed according to this Act and rules. Disposal of the cannabis waste rendered unusable may be delivered to a permitted solid waste facility for final disposition. Acceptable permitted solid waste facilities include, but are not limited to:

- Compostable mixed waste: Compost, anaerobic digester, or other facility with approval of the jurisdictional health department.
- No compostable mixed waste: Landfill, incinerator, or other facility with approval of the jurisdictional health department.

Cannabis Usage

The objective is for students to be able to define and explain the responsible use of cannabis and its psychological effects.

Health & Safety Concerns Of Cannabis Use

- Driving under the influence of cannabis is illegal and increases your risk of getting into a car crash.
- If you smoke or vape cannabis you may feel the effects right away, but it can take between 30 minutes and two hours to feel the effects of edibles. Edibles may have higher concentrations of tetrahydrocannabinol (THC, the active ingredient in cannabis). If you eat too much too fast, you are at higher risk for poisoning
- Smoke from cannabis contains many of the same toxins and chemicals found in tobacco smoke and inhaling it can increase your risk of developing lung problems.

| Keep Children Save | Physical And Psychological Effects | In The Event Of An Emergency |

Keep Children Safe

- Cannabis affects children more strongly than adults. Children are at higher risk for poisoning from cannabis, especially with edibles. Here are some safe practices you need to know.
- Store all cannabis products in a locked area. Make sure children cannot see or reach the locked area. Keep cannabis in the child-resistant packaging from the store.
- Never use cannabis around children.
- When you are using cannabis, make sure an adult who can look after your children is nearby.

Physical And Psychological Effects

- Altered senses (for example, seeing brighter colors)
- Difficulty with thinking and problem-solving
- Altered sense of time
- Changes in mood
- Impaired body movement
- Impaired memory
- Hallucinations (when taken in high doses)
- Delusions (when taken in high doses)
- Psychosis (when taken in high doses)

Test Your Knowledge

1. Every dispensary must designate at least one agent-in-charge who holds a dispensing organization agent identification card.

    a) True   b) False

2. Minors are permitted on the dispensing premises only if they are qualifying patients under the Compassionate Use of Medical Cannabis Program.

    a) True   b) False

3. The maximum allowable possession for Illinois residents is 60 grams of cannabis flower.

    a) True   b) False

4. Driving under the influence of cannabis is illegal in Illinois.

    a) True   b) False

5. All cannabis advertisements must not contain any misleading statements or promote overconsumption.

    a) True   b) False

Multiple-Choice Questions:

6. Which of the following is NOT an acceptable form of identification at a dispensary?
   a) Valid driver's license
   b) U.S. Passport
   c) Library card
   d) Armed Forces ID

7. What is the maximum amount of THC allowed in cannabis-infused products for non-Illinois residents?
   a) 100 milligrams
   b) 250 milligrams
   c) 500 milligrams
   d) 750 milligrams

8. Which of the following is a requirement for cannabis storage in a dispensary?
   a) Cannabis must be stored in open areas.
   b) All inventory must be secured in a restricted access area.
   c) Cannabis must be stored in clear containers.
   d) No restrictions apply to cannabis storage.

9. What is the minimum age a person must be to legally purchase cannabis in Illinois?
   a) 18
   b) 19
   c) 21
   d) 25

10. What action must an agent-in-charge take if an employee is terminated for diversion of product?
    a) Ignore it.
    b) Report it to the Department within 5 business days.
    c) Wait for the next audit to disclose it.
    d) Transfer the employee to another department.

Answer Sheet:

1. True
2. True
3. False (The limit is 30 grams)
4. True
5. True
6. c) Library card
7. b) 250 milligrams
8. b) All inventory must be secured in a restricted access area.
9. c) 21
10. b) Report it to the Department within 5 business days.

In The Event of Emergency

Call the local Poison Control Center at 1-800-222-1222. If you think a person needs immediate medical help, call 911!

Made in the USA
Columbia, SC
27 November 2024